Properties of
Matter
Teacher Supplement

1:1
Answers
IN GENESIS™

GOD'S
DESIGN®

4th Edition
Debbie & Richard Lawrence

God's Design® for Chemistry & Ecology
Properties of Matter Teacher Supplement

Reprinted July 2017

Fourth edition. Copyright © 2008, 2016 by Debbie & Richard Lawrence

ISBN: 978-1-62691-468-1

Published by Answers in Genesis, 2800 Bullittsburg Church Rd., Petersburg KY 41080

Book designer: Diane King
Editors: Gary Vaterlaus

Printed in China.

AnswersInGenesis.org • GodsDesign.com

Welcome to GOD'S DESIGN®

CHEMISTRY & ECOLOGY

God's Design for Chemistry & Ecology is a series that has been designed for use in teaching chemistry and ecology to elementary and middle school students. It is divided into three books: *Properties of Matter*, *Properties of Atoms and Molecules*, and *Properties of Ecosystems*. Each book has 35 lessons including a final project that ties all of the lessons together.

In addition to the lessons, special features in each book include biographical information on interesting people as well as fun facts to make the subject more fun.

Although this is a complete curriculum, the information included here is just a beginning, so please feel free to add to each lesson as you see fit. A resource guide is included in the appendices to help you find additional information and resources. A list of supplies needed is included at the beginning of each lesson, while a master list of all supplies needed for the entire series can be found in the appendices.

Answer keys for all review questions, worksheets, quizzes, and the final exam are included here. Reproducible student worksheets and tests may be found in the digital download that comes with the purchase of the curriculum. You may download these files from GodsDesign.com/ChemistryEcology.

If you prefer the files on a CD-ROM, you can order that from Answers in Genesis at an additional cost by calling 800-778-3390.

If you wish to get through all three books of the *Chemistry & Ecology* series in one year, you should plan on covering approximately three lessons per week. The time required for each lesson varies depending on how much additional information you want to include, but you can plan on about 45 minutes per lesson.

If you wish to cover the material in more depth, you may add additional information and take a longer period of time to cover all the material or you could choose to do only one or two of the books in the series as a unit study.

Why Teach Chemistry & Ecology?

Maybe you hate science or you just hate teaching it. Maybe you love science but don't quite know how to teach it to your children. Maybe science just doesn't seem as important as some of those other subjects you need to teach. Maybe you need a little motivation. If any of these descriptions fits you, then please consider the following.

It is not uncommon to question the need to teach your kids hands-on science in elementary school. We could argue that the knowledge gained in science will be needed later in life in order for your children to be more productive and well-rounded adults. We could argue that teaching your children science also teaches them logical and inductive thinking and reasoning skills, which are tools they will need to be more successful. We could argue that science is a necessity in this technological world in which we live. While all of these arguments are true, not one of them is the real reason that we should teach our children science. The most important reason to teach science in elementary school is to give your children an understanding that God is our Creator, and the Bible can be trusted. Teaching science from a creation perspective is one of the best ways to reinforce your children's faith in God and to help them counter the evolutionary propaganda they face every day.

God is the Master Creator of everything. His handiwork is all around us. Our Great Creator put in place all of the laws of physics, biology, and chemistry. These laws were put here for us to see His wisdom and power. In science, we see the hand of God at work more than in any other subject. Romans 1:20 says, "For since the creation of the world His invisible attributes are clearly seen, being understood by the things that are made, even His eternal power and Godhead, so that they [men] are without excuse." We need to help our children see God as Creator of the world around them so they will be able to recognize God and follow Him.

The study of chemistry helps us understand and appreciate the amazing way everything God created works together. The study of atoms and molecules and how different substances react with each other reveals an amazing design, even at the smallest level of life. Understanding the carbon, nitrogen, and water cycles helps our children see that God has a plan to keep everything working together. Learning about ecosystems reveals God's genius in nature.

It's fun to teach chemistry and ecology! It's interesting too. The elements of chemistry are all around us. Children naturally like to combine things to see what will happen. You just need to direct their curiosity.

Finally, teaching chemistry is easy. You won't have to try to find strange materials for experiments or do dangerous things to learn about chemistry. Chemistry is as close as your kitchen or your own body, and ecosystems are just outside your door.

How Do I Teach Science?

In order to teach any subject you need to understand how people learn. People learn in different ways. Most people, and children in particular, have a dominant or preferred learning style in which they absorb and retain information more easily.

If a student's dominant style is:

Auditory
He needs not only to hear the information but he needs to hear himself say it. This child needs oral presentation as well as oral drill and repetition.

Visual
She needs things she can see. This child responds well to flashcards, pictures, charts, models, etc.

Kinesthetic
He needs active participation. This child remembers best through games, hands-on activities, experiments, and field trips.

Also, some people are more relational while others are more analytical. The relational student needs to know why this subject is important, and how it will affect him personally. The analytical student, however, wants just the facts.

If you are trying to teach more than one student, you will probably have to deal with more than one learning style. Therefore, you need to present your lessons in several different ways so that each student can grasp and retain the information.

Grades 3–8

The first part of each lesson should be completed by all upper elementary and junior high students. This is the main part of the lesson containing a reading section, a hands-on activity that reinforces the ideas in the reading section (blue box), and a review section that provides review questions and application questions.

Grades 6–8

In addition, for middle school/junior high age students, we provide a "Challenge" section that contains more challenging material as well as additional activities and projects for older students (green box).

We have included periodic biographies to help your students appreciate the great men and women who have gone before us in the field of science.

We suggest a threefold approach to each lesson:

Introduce the topic

We give a brief description of the facts. Frequently you will want to add more information than the essentials given in this book. In addition to reading this section aloud (or having older children read it on their own), you may wish to do one or more of the following:

- Read a related book with your students.
- Write things down to help your visual learners.
- Give some history of the subject. We provide some historical sketches to help you, but you may want to add more.
- Ask questions to get your students thinking about the subject.

Make observations and do experiments

- Hands-on projects are suggested for each lesson. This part of each lesson may require help from the teacher.
- Have your students perform the activity by themselves whenever possible.

Review

- The "What did we learn?" section has review questions.
- The "Taking it further" section encourages students to
  - Draw conclusions
  - Make applications of what was learned
  - Add extended information to what was covered in the lesson
- The "FUN FACT" section adds fun or interesting information.

By teaching all three parts of the lesson, you will be presenting the material in a way that children with any learning style can both relate to and remember.

Also, this approach relates directly to the scientific method and will help your students think more scientifically. The *scientific method* is just a way to examine a subject logically and learn from it. Briefly, the steps of the scientific method are:

1. Learn about a topic.
2. Ask a question.
3. Make a hypothesis (a good guess).
4. Design an experiment to test your hypothesis.
5. Observe the experiment and collect data.
6. Draw conclusions. (Does the data support your hypothesis?)

Note: It's okay to have a "wrong hypothesis." That's how we learn. Be sure to help your students understand why they sometimes get a different result than expected.

Our lessons will help your students begin to approach problems in a logical, scientific way.

How Do I Teach Creation vs. Evolution?

We are constantly bombarded by evolutionary ideas about the earth in books, movies, museums, and even commercials. These raise many questions: Is a living being just a collection of chemicals? Did life begin as a random combination of chemicals? Can life be recreated in a laboratory? What does the chemical evidence tell us about the earth? The Bible answers these questions, and this book accepts the historical accuracy of the Bible as written. We believe this is the only way we can teach our children to trust that everything God says is true.

There are five common views of the origins of life and the age of the earth:

Historical biblical account	Progressive creation	Gap theory	Theistic evolution	Naturalistic evolution
Each day of creation in Genesis is a normal day of about 24 hours in length, in which God created everything that exists. The earth is only thousands of years old, as determined by the genealogies in the Bible.	The idea that God created various creatures to replace other creatures that died out over millions of years. Each of the days in Genesis represents a long period of time (day-age view) and the earth is billions of years old.	The idea that there was a long, long time between what happened in Genesis 1:1 and what happened in Genesis 1:2. During this time, the "fossil record" was supposed to have formed, and millions of years of earth history supposedly passed.	The idea that God used the process of evolution over millions of years (involving struggle and death) to bring about what we see today.	The view that there is no God and evolution of all life forms happened by purely naturalistic processes over billions of years.

Any theory that tries to combine the evolutionary time frame with creation presupposes that death entered the world before Adam sinned, which contradicts what God has said in His Word. The view that the earth (and its "fossil record") is hundreds of millions of years old damages the gospel message. God's completed creation was "very good" at the end of the sixth day (Genesis 1:31). Death entered this perfect paradise *after* Adam disobeyed God's command. It was the punishment for Adam's sin (Genesis 2:16–17; 3:19; Romans 5:12–19). Thorns appeared when God cursed the ground because of Adam's sin (Genesis 3:18).

The first animal death occurred when God killed at least one animal, shedding its blood, to make clothes for Adam and Eve (Genesis 3:21). If the earth's "fossil record" (filled with death, disease, and thorns) formed over millions of years before Adam appeared (and before he sinned), then death no longer would be the penalty for sin. Death, the "last enemy" (1 Corinthians 15:26), diseases (such as cancer), and thorns would instead be part of the original creation that God labeled "very good." No, it is clear that the "fossil record" formed sometime *after* Adam sinned—not many millions of years before. Most fossils were formed as a result of the worldwide Genesis Flood.

When viewed from a biblical perspective, the scientific evidence clearly supports a recent creation by God, and not naturalistic evolution and millions of years. The volume of evidence supporting the biblical creation account is substantial and cannot be adequately covered in this book. If you would like more information on this topic, please see the resource guide in the appendices. To help get you started, just a few examples of evidence supporting biblical creation are given below:

Evolutionary Myth: Life evolved from non-life when chemicals randomly combined together to produce amino acids and then proteins that produced living cells.

The Truth: The chemical requirements for DNA and proteins to line up just right to create life could not have happened through purely natural processes. The process of converting DNA information into proteins requires at least 75 different protein molecules. But each and every one of these 75 proteins must be synthesized in the first place by the process in which they themselves are involved. How could the process begin without the presence of all the necessary proteins? Could all 75 proteins have arisen by chance in just the right place at just the right time? Dr. Gary Parker says this is like the chicken and the egg problem. The obvious conclusion is that both the DNA and proteins must have been functional from the beginning, otherwise life could not exist. The best explanation for the existence of these proteins and DNA is that God created them.

Gary Parker, *Creation: Facts of Life* (Master Books, 2006), pp. 20–43.

Evolutionary Myth: Stanley Miller created life in a test tube, thus demonstrating that the early earth had the conditions necessary for life to begin.

The Truth: Although Miller was able to create amino acids from raw chemicals in his famous experiment, he did not create anything close to life or even the ingredients of life. There are four main problems with Miller's experiment. First, he left out oxygen because he knew that oxygen corrodes and destroys amino acids very quickly. However, rocks found in every layer of the earth indicate that oxygen has always been a part of the earth's atmosphere. Second, Miller included ammonia gas and methane gas. Ammonia gas would not have been present in any large quantities because it would have been dissolved in the oceans. And there is no indication in any of the rock layers that methane has ever been a part of the earth's atmosphere. Third, Miller used a spark of electricity to cause the amino acids to form, simulating lightning. However, this spark more quickly destroyed the amino acids than built them up, so to keep the amino acids from being destroyed, Miller used specially designed equipment to siphon off the amino acids before they could be destroyed. This is not what would have happened in nature. And finally, although Miller did produce amino acids, they were not the kinds of amino acids that are needed for life as we know it. Most of the acids were ones that actually break down proteins, not build them up.

Mike Riddle, "Can Natural Processes Explain the Origin of Life," in *The New Answers Book 2*, Ken Ham, ed. (Master Books, 2008). See also www.answersingenesis.org/go/origin.

Evolutionary Myth: Living creatures are just a collection of chemicals.

The Truth: It is true that cells are made of specific chemicals. However, a dead animal is made of the same chemicals as it was when it was living, but it cannot become alive again. What makes the chemicals into a living creature is the result of the organization of the substances, not just the substances themselves. Dr. Parker again uses an example. An airplane is made up of millions of non-flying parts; however, it can fly because of the design and organization of those parts. Similarly, plants and animals are alive because God created the chemicals in a specific way for them to be able to live. A collection of all the right parts is not life.

Evolutionary Myth: Chemical evidence points to an earth that is billions of years old.

The Truth: Much of the chemical evidence actually points to a young earth. For example, radioactive decay in the earth's crust produces helium atoms that rise to the surface and enter the atmosphere. Assuming that the rate of helium production has always been constant (an evolutionary assumption), the maximum age for the atmosphere could only be 2 million years.[1] This is much younger than the 4+ billion years claimed by evolutionists. And there are many ideas that could explain the presence of helium that would indicate a much younger age than 2 million years. Similarly, salt accumulates in the ocean over time. Evolutionists claim that life evolved in a salty ocean 3–4 billion years ago. If this were true and the salt has continued to accumulate over billions of years, the ocean would be too salty for anything to live in by now. Using the most conservative possible values (those that would give the oldest possible age for the oceans), scientists have calculated that the ocean must be less than 62 million years. That number is based on the assumption that nothing has affected the rate at which the salt is accumulating. However, the Genesis Flood would have drastically altered the amount of salt in the ocean, dissolving much sodium from land rocks.[2] Thus, the chemical evidence does not support an earth that is billions of years old.

[1] Don DeYoung, *Thousands…not billions* (Master Books, 2005).
[2] John D. Morris, *The Young Earth* (Master Books, 2007), pp. 83–87. See also www.answersingenesis.org/go/salty.

Despite the claims of many scientists, if you examine the evidence objectively, it is obvious that evolution and millions of years have not been proven. You can be confident that if you teach that what the Bible says is true, you won't go wrong. Instill in your student a confidence in the truth of the Bible in all areas. If scientific thought seems to contradict the Bible, realize that scientists often make mistakes, but God does not lie. At one time scientists believed that the earth was the center of the universe, that living things could spring from non-living things, and that blood-letting was good for the body. All of these were believed to be scientific facts but have since been disproved, but the Word of God remains true. If we use modern "science" to interpret the Bible, what will happen to our faith in God's Word when scientists change their theories yet again?

Integrating the Seven C's

The Seven C's is a framework in which all of history, and the future to come, can be placed. As we go through our daily routines we may not understand how the details of life connect with the truth that we find in the Bible. This is also the case for students. When discussing the importance of the Bible you may find yourself telling students that the Bible is relevant in everyday activities. But how do we help the younger generation see that? The Seven C's are intended to help.

The Seven C's can be used to develop a biblical worldview in students, young or old. Much more than entertaining stories and religious teachings, the Bible has real connections to our everyday life. It may be hard, at first, to see how many connections there are, but with practice, the daily relevance of God's Word will come alive. Let's look at the Seven C's of History and how each can be connected to what the students are learning.

Creation

God perfectly created the heavens, the earth, and all that is in them in six normal-length days around 6,000 years ago.

This teaching is foundational to a biblical worldview and can be put into the context of any subject. In science, the amazing design that we see in nature—whether in the veins of a leaf or the complexity of your hand—is all the handiwork of God. Virtually all of the lessons in *God's Design for Science* can be related to God's creation of the heavens and earth.

Other contexts include:

Natural laws—any discussion of a law of nature naturally leads to God's creative power.

DNA and information—the information in every living thing was created by God's supreme intelligence.

Mathematics—the laws of mathematics reflect the order of the Creator.

Biological diversity—the distinct kinds of animals that we see were created during the Creation Week, not as products of evolution.

Art—the creativity of man is demonstrated through various art forms.

History—all time scales can be compared to the biblical time scale extending back about 6,000 years.

Ecology—God has called mankind to act as stewards over His creation.

Corruption

After God completed His perfect creation, Adam disobeyed God by eating the forbidden fruit. As a result, sin and death entered the world, and the world has been in decay since that time. This point is evident throughout the world that we live in. The struggle for survival in animals, the death of loved ones, and the violence all around us are all examples of the corrupting influence of sin.

Other contexts include:

Genetics—the mutations that lead to diseases, cancer, and variation within populations are the result of corruption.

Biological relationships—predators and parasites result from corruption.

History—wars and struggles between mankind, exemplified in the account of Cain and Abel, are a result of sin.

Catastrophe

God was grieved by the wickedness of mankind and judged this wickedness with a global Flood. The Flood covered the entire surface of the earth and killed all air-breathing creatures that were not aboard the Ark. The eight people and the animals aboard the Ark replenished the earth after God delivered them from the catastrophe.

The catastrophe described in the Bible would naturally leave behind much evidence. The studies of geology and of the biological diversity of animals on the planet are two of the most obvious applications of this event. Much of scientific understanding is based on how a scientist views the events of the Genesis Flood.

Other contexts include:

Biological diversity—all of the birds, mammals, and other air-breathing animals have populated the earth from the original kinds which left the Ark.

Geology—the layers of sedimentary rock seen in road-cuts, canyons, and other geologic features are testaments to the global Flood.

Geography—features like mountains, valleys, and plains were formed as the floodwaters receded.

Physics—rainbows are a perennial sign of God's faithfulness and His pledge to never flood the entire earth again.

Fossils—Most fossils are a result of the Flood rapidly burying plants and animals.

Plate tectonics—the rapid movement of the earth's plates likely accompanied the Flood.

Global warming/Ice Age—both of these items are likely a result of the activity of the Flood. The warming we are experiencing today has been present since the peak of the Ice Age (with variations over time).

Confusion

God commanded Noah and his descendants to spread across the earth. The refusal to obey this command and the building of the tower at Babel caused God to judge this sin. The common language of the people was confused and they spread across the globe as groups with a common language. All people are truly of "one blood" as descendants of Noah and, originally, Adam.

The confusion of the languages led people to scatter across the globe. As people settled in new areas, the traits they carried with them became concentrated in those populations. Traits like dark skin were beneficial in the tropics while other traits benefited populations in northern climates, and distinct people groups, not races, developed.

Other contexts include:

Genetics—the study of human DNA has shown that there is little difference in the genetic makeup of the so-called "races."

Languages—there are about seventy language groups from which all modern languages have developed.

Archaeology—the presence of common building structures, like pyramids, around the world confirms the biblical account.

Literature—recorded and oral records tell of similar events relating to the Flood and the dispersion at Babel.

Christ

God did not leave mankind without a way to be redeemed from its sinful state. The Law was given to Moses to show how far away man is from God's standard of perfection. Rather than the sacrifices, which only covered sins, people needed a Savior to take away their sin. This was accomplished when Jesus Christ came to earth to live a perfect life and, by that obedience, was able to be the sacrifice to satisfy God's wrath for all who believe.

The deity of Christ and the amazing plan that was set forth before the foundation of the earth is the core of Christian doctrine. The earthly life of Jesus was the fulfillment of many prophecies and confirms the truthfulness of the Bible. His miracles and presence in human form demonstrate that God is both intimately concerned with His creation and able to control it in an absolute way.

Other contexts include:

Psychology—popular secular psychology teaches of the inherent goodness of man, but Christ has lived the only perfect life. Mankind needs a Savior to redeem it from its unrighteousness.

Biology—Christ's virgin birth demonstrates God's sovereignty over nature.

Physics—turning the water into wine and the feeding of the five thousand demonstrate Christ's deity and His sovereignty over nature.

History—time is marked (in the western world) based on the birth of Christ despite current efforts to change the meaning.

Art—much art is based on the life of Christ and many of the masters are known for these depictions, whether on canvas or in music.

Cross

Because God is perfectly just and holy, He must punish sin. The sinless life of Jesus Christ was offered as a substitutionary sacrifice for all of those who will repent and put their faith in the Savior. After His death on the Cross, He defeated death by rising on the third day and is now seated at the right hand of God.

The events surrounding the Crucifixion and Ressurection have a most significant place in the life of Christians. Though there is no way to scientifically prove the Ressurection, there is likewise no way to prove the stories of evolutionary history. These are matters of faith founded in the truth of God's Word and His character. The eyewitness testimony of over 500 people and the written Word of God provide the basis for our belief.

Other contexts include:

Biology—the biological details of the Crucifixion can be studied alongside the anatomy of the human body.

History—the use of Crucifixion as a method of punishment was short-lived in historical terms and not known at the time it was prophesied.

Art—the Crucifixion and Resurrection have inspired many wonderful works of art.

Consummation

God, in His great mercy, has promised that He will restore the earth to its original state—a world without death, suffering, war, and disease. The corruption introduced by Adam's sin will be removed. Those who have repented and put their trust in the completed work of Christ on the Cross will experience life in this new heaven and earth. We will be able to enjoy and worship God forever in a perfect place.

This future event is a little more difficult to connect with academic subjects. However, the hope of a life in God's presence and in the absence of sin can be inserted in discussions of human conflict, disease, suffering, and sin in general.

Other contexts include:

History—in discussions of war or human conflict the coming age offers hope.

Biology—the violent struggle for life seen in the predator-prey relationships will no longer taint the earth.

Medicine—while we struggle to find cures for diseases and alleviate the suffering of those enduring the effects of the Curse, we ultimately place our hope in the healing that will come in the eternal state.

The preceding examples are given to provide ideas for integrating the Seven C's of History into a broad range of curriculum activities. We would recommend that you give your students, and yourself, a better understanding of the Seven C's framework by using AiG's *Answers for Kids* curriculum. The first seven lessons of this curriculum cover the Seven C's and will establish a solid understanding of the true history, and future, of the universe. Full lesson plans, activities, and student resources are provided in the curriculum set.

We also offer bookmarks displaying the Seven C's and a wall chart. These can be used as visual cues for the students to help them recall the information and integrate new learning into its proper place in a biblical worldview.

Even if you use other curricula, you can still incorporate the Seven C's teaching into those. Using this approach will help students make firm connections between biblical events and every aspect of the world around them, and they will begin to develop a truly biblical worldview and not just add pieces of the Bible to what they learn in "the real world."

Unit 1
Experimental Science

1   Introduction toExperimental Science
Learning about Matter

Supply list

Wooden spoon

Metal spoon

Ruler

Pencil

Butter knife

Large cup hot water

Butter or margarine

Stopwatch

Copy of "Conducting Heat Experiment" worksheet

What did we learn?

- What is matter? **Anything that has mass and takes up space.**

- What do chemists study? **They study the way matter reacts with other matter and the environment.**

- What is an experiment? **A controlled test.**

Taking it further

- Why is it important to study chemistry? **Chemistry is important to every other area of science.**

- What are two things you need to know before conducting an experiment? **The purpose and what you expect to happen.**

2   The Scientific Method
How do scientists do it?

Supply list

3 empty plastic bottles

Masking tape

Yeast

Marker

Sugar

Cloth tape measure or string

Copy of "Scientific Method" worksheet

Molasses

3 identical balloons

Thermometer

Measuring cup and spoons

Scientific Method worksheet

- **Taste, color, and texture are all affected by the sweetener used, so even if molasses produces the most gas, you may not like the way it makes your bread taste or look.**

What did we learn?

- What is the overall job of a scientist? **To systematically study the physical world.**

- What are some areas that cannot be studied by science? **Morality, religion, philosophy, history.**

- What are the five steps of the scientific method? **Learn or observe, ask a question, make a hypothesis, design and perform a test, check the results, and draw conclusions.**

Taking it further

- Why was it necessary to have bottle number 1 in the experiment? **Bottle 1 had only water and yeast. This is called a control. It shows how much gas was produced without a sweetener, so you can tell exactly how much** gas was caused by adding the sugar and molasses in the other bottles.

- What other sweeteners could you try in your experiment? **Honey, corn syrup, fruit juice.**

- What sweeteners were used in the bread at your house? **Look at the ingredients list on the package if** you do not bake your own bread. Possible answers are sugar, corn syrup, and honey.

- Why do you think the company used that sweetener? **Reasons vary, but amount of gas produced, cost, color, and taste are all important factors in why companies use the ingredients they do.**

 # Tools of Science

Using the right tool for the job

Supply list

Thermometer

Masking tape

Liquid measuring cup

Marker

Small box

Copy of "Scientific Tools" worksheet

Tennis ball

2 cups

Metric ruler or meter stick

Digital stop watch

Supplies for Challenge (if available):

Microscope

Prepared slides

Telescope

Scientific Tools worksheet

- **Answers to "Conclusion" questions: Quantitative measurements are more accurate. In general, quantitative measurements are more useful; however, this depends on what you are trying to accomplish. It is not always necessary to make quantitative measurements. You may only need to know if something is warm or melted without having to measure its temperature, for example.**

What did we learn?

- What is the main thing a scientist does as he/she studies the physical world? **Makes observations.**

- What are the two types of observations that a scientist can make? **Qualitative observations are ones made by the 5 senses without numerical data. Quantitative measurements or observations are made using instruments that generate numerical or other objective data.**

- What is the main problem with qualitative measurements? **The observations may vary from person to person because we each perceive things differently.**

- What are some scientific tools used for quantitative observations? **Balance, graduated cylinder, thermometer, meter stick, spectrometer, etc.**

Taking it further

- What qualitative observations might you make when observing the experiment in lesson 1? **You might observe that the metal spoon is hotter than a wooden spoon or that butter begins to melt faster or slower on certain items.**

- What quantitative observations might you make when observing the experiment in lesson 1? **You might measure the temperature of the water and the temperature of each item. You did measure the length of time it took for the butter to begin to melt on each item. You could also measure the length of time it takes for the butter to completely melt on each item.**

4 The Metric System

Standard Units

Supply list

Measuring cup (metric)   Pencil
Meter stick   Paper clip

Using Metric Units

a. **1 liter**   d. **6 centimeters**

b. **20,000 grams**   e. **500 decigrams**

c. **4000 meters**

What did we learn?

- What are some units used to measure length in the Old English/American measuring system? **Inch, foot, yard, mile, rod, hand, span.**
- What is the unit used to measure length in the metric system? **Meter.**
- What metric unit is used for measuring mass? **Gram.**
- What metric unit is used for measuring liquid volume? **Liter.**
- Why do scientists use the metric system instead of another measuring system? **It is easy to convert from** one unit to another, and it is based on only a few basic units. In fact, liters and grams are actually based on the meter. For example, the liter is actually the volume of a cube that is .1 X .1 X .1 meters and a gram is the mass of 1/1000 of a liter, or one cubic centimeter, of water.

Taking it further

- What metric unit would be best to use to measure the distance across a room? **Meters would be the best unit.**
- What metric unit would you use to measure the distance from one town to another? **The distance would be a very large number if you used meters, so kilometers would be a better choice.**
- What metric unit would you use to measure the width of a hair? **This is much smaller than a meter, so a millimeter or micrometer would be a better choice.**

Challenge: Measuring Scales

- **Earthquakes are measured by the Richter scale which measures the intensity of the quake and the Mercalli scale which measures the damage done by the earthquake.**

QUIZ 1 Experimental Science

Lessons 1–4

Number the steps of the scientific method in the correct order.

A.   _2_   Ask a question.

B.   _1_   Learn about something/Make observations.

C.   _6_   Share your results.

D.   _4_   Design a test and perform it.

E.   _3_   Make a hypothesis.

F.   _5_   Check your results/Is your hypothesis right?

Mark each statement as either True or False.

1.   _F_   You must always have a correct hypothesis.

2.   _T_   It is important to control variables in your experiments.

3.   _F_   Qualitative observations always use numbers.

4.   _T_   Quantitative observations can be more useful to scientists than qualitative observations.

5.   _T_   It is usually easier to make conversions between units in the metric system than in the Old English/American system.

6.   _T_   A millimeter is smaller than a meter.

7.   _F_   A graduated cylinder should be used to measure mass.

8. _T_ God has established laws to govern how chemicals react with each other.

9. _F_ Science can always tell us why things happen.

10. _F_ Matter has no mass.

11. Describe what chemistry is the study of. **Chemistry is the study of matter and how it reacts.**

Challenge questions

Short answer:

12. Is the measurement of the intensity of light from a distant star origins science or observation science? **Observation.**

13. Is the use of distant starlight to date the universe an example of origins science or observation science? **Origins.**

14. Why shouldn't you look through the eyepiece while lowering the objective on a microscope? **You could run the lens into the slide, causing damage.**

15. How are microscopes similar to telescopes? **They both use lenses to make an image larger.**

16. How are microscopes different from telescopes? **Microscopes only use lenses; telescopes sometimes use mirrors too; microscopes are used to view tiny objects; telescopes are used to view far away objects.**

Match the scale with what phenomenon it describes.

17. _C_ Mohs scale

18. _A_ Fujita scale

19. _E_ Saffir-Simpson scale

20. _B_ Beaufort scale

21. _D_ Richter scale

22. _F_ Mercalli scale

Measuring Matter

Mass versus Weight

What's the difference?

Supply list

Ruler with holes in it to fit a 3-ring binder

Thin rubber band | 25 pennies
String | Tape
Paper | Several paper clips
2 pencils | Single-hole punch
3 paper cups

Supplies for Challenge:

Copy of "Mass & Weight Units" worksheet

What did we learn?

- What is the difference between mass and weight? **Mass is the amount of material there is in an object and weight is how much gravity pulls down on an object.**

- How do you measure mass? **By using a balance to compare an object to a known mass.**

- How do you measure weight? **By using a spring scale that is marked for known weights.**

Taking it further

- What would your weight be in outer space? **Nearly zero because there is very little gravity in space.**

- What would your mass be in outer space? **The same as it is on earth.**

- Name a place in the universe where you might go to increase your weight without changing your mass. **Any of the larger planets such as Jupiter or Saturn. Of course, you cannot really go there and you could not survive there if you could, but the gravity is much higher there than on earth so you would weigh much more there.**

Challenge: Mass & Weight Units worksheet

1. _Weight_   5. _Weight_   9. _Mass_
2. _Mass_   6. _Mass_   10. _Mass_
3. _Mass_   7. _Weight_   11. _Mass_
4. _Weight_   8. _Mass_   12. _Weight_

Conservation of Mass

Where does it go?

Supply list

2 paper cups | 3 or 4 sugar cubes
Balance from lesson 5 | Spoon

Supplies for Challenge:

Bottle | Vinegar
Gram scale | Baking soda

Balloon
Copy of "Conservation of Mass" worksheet

What did we learn?

- What is the law of conservation of mass? **Matter cannot be created nor destroyed. It can change form, but it does not go away.**

- How is the mass of water changed when it turns to ice? **It does not change.**

Taking it further

- If you start with 10 grams of water and you boil it until there is no water left in the pan, what happened to the water? **The 10 grams of water turned into 10 grams of steam and entered the air, but it did not disappear or go away.**

- Why is the law of conservation of mass important to understanding the beginning of the world? **It shows that matter cannot create itself or be created by any-** thing in nature. Therefore it had to be created by something outside of nature. We know from the Bible that all matter was created by God.

Challenge: Conservation of Mass worksheet

- **The mass of the bottle, liquid, and paper is less after the reaction because some of the matter turned into gas and escaped from the bottle. The missing mass is in the CO_2 molecules. Mass should not change when using the balloon, but if it does, it is likely that some gas escaped around the edge of the balloon.**

Volume

How much space does it take up?

Supply list

Meter stick	Metric ruler
Small box	Liquid measuring cup
Small object (eraser, toy, etc.)	

Supplies for Challenge:

Box of dry food	Ice cream cone
Tennis ball	Die (6-sided)
Can of food	
Copy of "Calculating Volume" worksheet	

What did we learn?

- What is volume? **The amount of room or space something occupies.**

- Does air have volume? **Yes, even though you can't see it, it still takes up space. It expands to fill up the avail-** able space. Think about a balloon. The air forces the balloon to expand; visibly showing how much room the air is taking up.

Taking it further

- If you have a cube that is 10 centimeters on each side, what would its volume be? **10 cm x 10 cm x 10 cm = 1000 cubic centimeters.**

- Why is volume important to a scientist? **The volume of matter can be related to many things that scientists are interested in. For example, the volume that a certain amount of fuel occupies determines how a vehicle will be designed.**

Challenge: Calculating Volume worksheet

- **Answers will vary. Be sure student correctly used each formula.**

Density

Does it feel heavy?

Supply list

Ping-pong ball	Paper clips
Golf ball	Liquid measuring cup
Balance from lesson 5	
Pennies	

Supplies for Challenge:

Metal spoon	Plastic cap
Marble	Quarter
Eraser	
Copy of "Density Experiment" worksheet	

Measuring Density

- How did the mass of the golf ball compare to the mass of the ping-pong ball? **It should be significantly more.**
- How did the volume of the golf ball compare to the volume of the ping-pong ball? **It should be about the same.**
- Which ball has a higher density? **The golf ball.**

What did we learn?

- What is the definition of density? **The mass of an object divided by its volume.**
- If two substances with the same volume have different densities how can you tell which one is the densest? **If they have the same volume, the one that is heavier will have the higher density.**

Taking it further

- If you have two unknown substances that both appear to be silvery colored, how can you tell if they are the same material? **Measure their densities. Platinum has a density of 21.45 g/cc, lead is 11.3 g/cc and aluminum is 2.7 g/cc. This may give you a clue to the material's identity.**
- If two objects have the same density and the same size what will be true about their masses? **They will have the same mass.**
- If you suspect that someone is trying to pass off a gold plated bar of lead as a solid gold bar, how can you test your theory? **Measure the density of the bar. Gold has a density of 19.3 g/cc while lead has a density of 11.3 g/cc. Even though lead may seem heavy, it is not as dense as gold.**
- Why does the ping-pong ball have a lower density than the golf ball? **It is filled with air. Air is very light compared to most substances. The golf ball is filled with plastic, rubber, or other solid materials.**

Challenge: Density Experiment worksheet

- **Answers will vary. Be sure student used the correct procedure to calculate density.**

Buoyancy

It floats!

Supply list

Rubbing alcohol   Modeling clay

Vegetable oil   2 cups

Popcorn (including some unpopped kernels)

Supplies for Challenge:

Plastic tub   Water

Sink   Helium balloon (optional)

Tape

Metal objects (wrenches, etc.) that fit in the tub

Testing Buoyancy

- Activity 1: Which shape floats? **If you formed the boat carefully, you should be able to get it to float, whereas the ball will probably sink.**
- Activity 2: What did you observe happening? **You should see the fluffy pieces rise to the top and the unpopped kernels sink to the bottom. The kernels are** denser than the popped pieces. The popped pieces take up more space, but have the same amount of matter as the kernels so they are less dense and thus rise to the top.
- Activity 3: What happened to the oil in each cup? **You should have observed that the oil floated on the top of the water but sank to the bottom of the alcohol.**
- Why did the oil float in one cup but sink in the other? **Oil is less dense than water but more dense than alcohol. The oil is buoyant in the water but not in the alcohol.**

What did we learn?

- What is buoyancy? **The ability to float.**
- If something is buoyant, what does that tell you about its density compared to that of the substance in which it floats? **It means that the object's density is less than the density of the substance that it is floating on.**
- Are you buoyant in water? **Probably, especially if you are holding your breath.**

Taking it further

- What are some substances that are buoyant in water besides you? **Ivory soap, a leaf, paper, oil, etc.**

- Based on what you observed, which is denser, water or alcohol? **Water is denser. Oil will float on the water but sinks in the alcohol.**

- Why is a foam swimming tube or a foam life ring able to keep a person afloat in the water? **Foam is a material that has air trapped in it so it is not very dense. Even with the person's weight/mass added to it, the foam object's density remains lower than the density of the water.**

- Why is it important to life that ice is less dense than water? **Otherwise rivers and lakes would freeze from the bottom up, and no life could survive in them.**

QUIZ 2

Measuring Matter

Lessons 5–9

Match the term with its definition.

1. _C_ The amount of a substance
2. _H_ How strongly something is pulled on by gravity
3. _A_ Matter cannot be created or destroyed
4. _D_ How much space matter occupies
5. _B_ How much mass is in a particular volume
6. _G_ The ability for one substance to float in another
7. _F_ Used to measure mass
8. _E_ Used to measure weight
9. _J_ A material that is denser than lead
10. _I_ Only common material to become less dense when frozen

Short answer:

11. Explain how the water you drink today could be the same water a dinosaur drank thousands of years ago. **Water is recycled. After a dinosaur drank water it exhaled some water into the atmosphere. That water has been recycled through the water cycle for thousands of years.**

12. Explain what happens to nitrogen in the soil and in plants that demonstrates conservation of mass. **Nitrogen is absorbed by plants, eaten by animals, then returned to the soil when the plant or animal dies. It does not get used up.**

13. If an object floats in one liquid but sinks in another, what does that tell you about the densities of the two liquids? **The first liquid is denser than the second.**

14. How would you determine the volume of a toy car? **Use the displacement method.**

15. How are buoyancy and density related? **One substance is buoyant in another if it is less dense than the other substance.**

Challenge questions

Short answer:

16. What are two units for measuring mass? **Grams, slugs.**

17. What are two units for measuring weight? **Newtons, pounds.**

18. If you perform an experiment and the mass of the resulting substance is less than the mass of what you started with, what is one likely explanation? **It is likely that a gas was produced and escaped from the experiment. A nuclear reaction converts a small amount of mass into energy.**

19. Which is likely to be more dense, a one inch cube of steel or a one inch cube of wood? **Steel is denser than wood.**

20. If you are traveling in a car with a helium balloon and the driver suddenly puts on the brakes, what will happen to your body and what will happen to the balloon? **Your momentum will carry your body forward as the car suddenly slows down. It will also carry air molecules forward. Helium is lighter than the air so the balloon will move backward to take the place of the air molecules.**

States of Matter

Physical & Chemical Properties

Is it something new?

Supply list

Sauce pan	Lemon juice
Ice	Baking soda
Salt	Cup

Supplies for Challenge:

Copy of "Physical or Chemical Properties" worksheet

Physical & Chemical Changes

1. **Ice melting is a physical change; no other elements were added to the water and it just changed state without becoming something else. Salt dissolving in water is also a physical change.**
2. **The salt molecules are moved farther away from each other, but they are not combined with the water to form something new.**
3. **The fact that the salt remains behind is a good clue that it did not react with the water.**
4. **The lemon juice and baking soda is a chemical change. The fact that bubbles are generated is a clue that some kind of gas is being generated, indicating a new substance being formed.**

What did we learn?

- What are some physical properties of matter? **These could include color, texture, temperature, density, mass, state, etc.**
- What is a chemical change? **When two or more substances combine to form a different substance.**
- Give an example of a chemical change. **There are innumerable examples. Some common chemical changes that might be mentioned include photosynthesis, hydrogen and oxygen combining to form water, vinegar and baking soda combining to form carbon dioxide, yeast turning sugar into carbon dioxide, rust, digesting food, etc.**

Taking it further

- How can you determine if a change in matter is a physical change or a chemical change? **Find out if the ending matter is the same type of matter as what you started with. Chemical changes often involve release of energy such as heat, light, or sound.**
- Diamond and quartz appear to have very similar physical properties. They are both clear crystalline substances. However, diamond is much harder than quartz. How would this affect their effectiveness as tips for drill bits? **The quartz-tipped drill would quickly wear down and be ineffective. Diamond-tipped drills are very hard and very effective at drilling through nearly any other substance. It is important to understand physical properties of matter as well as chemical properties.**

Challenge: Physical or Chemical Properties worksheet

1. _P_ Liquid water becoming steam (**Steam is still water**)
2. _C_ Flavor/taste (**Texture contributes to taste but most of the flavor is detected through chemical reactions in the taste buds**)
3. _C_ Burning of wood/fire (**The wood and oxygen combine to form ash, water, and carbon dioxide. Heat and light are released during this chemical reaction.**)
4. _P_ Filling a balloon with air (**The balloon changes shape but is still a balloon, and the air is still air.**)
5. _P_ Softness (**Softness is a physical characteristic of the object.**)
6. _P_ Making ice cream (**The sugar & milk mixture is frozen but does not become something else.**)
7. _C_ Digesting food (**Some physical aspects but is primarily chemical.**)
8. _P_ Straightening a paper clip (**Only the shape is changed. No new materials are formed.**)

9. _P_ Cloud formation (**Water vapor condenses to form water liquid—physical change only.**)

10. _C_ Rust on a piece of iron (**Oxygen combines with water and iron to form iron oxide—rust.**)

11. _C_ Separation of water into hydrogen and oxygen gases (**New materials are formed.**)

12. _P_ Dissolving sugar in water (**The water is still water and the sugar is still sugar, it is just broken into very small pieces and mixed up with the water.**)

13. _C_ Photosynthesis (**Water and carbon dioxide combine to form sugar and oxygen.**)

14. _C_ Bacteria decaying dead plant matter (**Complex tissues are broken down into basic elements by the bacteria.**)

15. _P_ Shine/luster (**Luster is determined by what the substance is. It is a physical characteristic.**)

16. _C_ A cake rising in the oven (**This is really both. Gas is produced as chemical reactions take place. There is also a physical element of the batter being stretched by the gas.**)

17. _P_ Cutting a piece of wood (**The wood is not changed into something else just because it becomes smaller.**)

18. _C_ Bread rising (**Like the cake is it both chemical and physical.**)

19. _P_ Hardness (**This is a physical characteristic dependent on the material.**)

20. _P or C_ Making perfume (**Depends on the process.**)

11 States of Matter

Phase Changes

Supply list

Ice	Ice tray
Small saucepan	Access to stove and freezer
Hand mirror	

Supplies for Challenge:

Jar	Water
Marker	

Observing Phase Changes

- How does it feel? **Hard, cold, smooth.**
- How does the liquid compare to the solid? **It is warmer, can be moved easier, wet.**
- What did you notice as the water began to boil? **Little bubbles came up from the bottom of the pan. Steam rose from the water.**
- How does the water on the mirror feel? **Cool and wet.**
- How does the water look and feel now? **Cold, hard, smooth.**

What did we learn?

- What are the three physical states of most matter? **Solid, liquid, gas.**
- What is the name for each phase change? **Solid to liquid is melting, liquid to gas is evaporation, gas to liquid is condensation, liquid to solid is freezing, and for those substances that can go directly from solid to gas or gas to solid, the phase change is called sublimation.**
- What is required to bring about a phase change in a substance? **The addition or removal of energy—primarily in the form of heat.**

Taking it further

- Name several substances that are solid at room temperature. **The answers are endless. Some ideas include metals, wood, plastic, many foods, people, animals, etc.**
- Name several substances that are liquid at room temperature. **Some ideas include water, juice, tea, honey, rubbing alcohol, and syrup.**
- Name several substances that are gas at room temperature. **Some ideas include air, nitrogen, oxygen, hydrogen, carbon dioxide, carbon monoxide, propane, and natural gas.**

12 Solids

Hard as a rock

Supply list

Wooden block	Metal spoon
Honey	Silly putty
Rock	

Testing For Solids

1. Does it take up the same amount of room if you put it in another container? **All five substances will take up the same amount of space. This is a characteristic of solids and liquids because they do not expand to fill their containers.**

2. Is it denser than air, or does it float in air? **None of these objects floats, so they are all denser than air. Being dense is a characteristic of most solids and liquids.**

3. Does its shape stay the same if I move it or put it in another container? **Honey quickly flows to take on the shape of its container so it is not a solid. The silly putty is trickier. You have to let it sit for a long time before you see it start to flow outward. But if you leave it long enough it will also take on the shape of its container. It is a very thick liquid. The other substances keep their shape.**

4. Is it a solid? **If you answered yes to all three questions, the object is a solid. Honey and silly putty are** not solids because they do not keep their shapes, but wood, rocks and spoons are solid.

What did we learn?

- What are three characteristics of solids? **They keep their shape, they have a definite volume, they are denser than most liquids and gases, they have lower kinetic energy than liquids or gases, and their molecules are closely packed together.**

- How do large crystals form in solids? **If the liquid cools down very slowly, the molecules may be able to line up in regular patterns to make crystals.**

- What state is the most common for the basic elements? **Nearly 90% of the elements are solids.**

Taking it further

- Is gelatin a solid or a liquid? **Gels such as gelatin are neither a solid nor a liquid. Instead they are a liquid that is suspended within a solid structure. Therefore, they have characteristics of both solids and liquids. They can be made to move like a liquid, yet hold their shape if left alone. Other phases can be suspended within each other as well. A foam is a gas that is suspended in a liquid. Smoke is solid that is suspended in a gas. Fog is a liquid that is suspended in a gas.**

13 Liquids

Can you pour it?

Supply list

Water	Dish soap
Hand lotion	Honey
Vegetable Oil	Baking sheet
Copy of "Viscosity" worksheet	

Supplies for Challenge:

Cup of water

What did we learn?

- Which has more kinetic energy, a solid or a liquid? **A liquid.**

- What shape does a liquid have? **The shape of its container.**

- What is viscosity? **A measure of how strongly the liquid's molecules are attracted to each other.**

Taking it further

- How is a liquid similar to a solid? **Both a solid and a liquid are much denser than a gas, both have a definite volume that can be measured, the molecules of both are close together.**

- How is a liquid different from a solid? **Its molecules move freely over one another and its shape changes when you put it in a different container.**

- How would you change a solid into a liquid? **You melt it by adding more energy, usually in the form of heat.**

14 Gases

Lighter than air?

Supply list

2 tennis balls (Note: place 1 of the balls in the freezer about 30 minutes before you plan to use it.)

Supplies for Challenge:

Perfume   Step ladder

Cup

Observing Air Pressure

- Why does a ball bounce? **It is because the air molecules inside the ball are pressing against the inside of the ball. So when a ball hits the floor, the molecules inside it push back against the floor, causing the ball to bounce up.**

- Do gas molecules move faster when they are warm or when they are cold? **The warmer the molecules are, the faster they will be moving.**

- Which ball bounced highest? **The warm ball will bounce higher.**

- Why does the warmer ball bounce higher? **The molecules inside the ball are moving faster so more particles collide with the inside of the ball when it hits the floor. This gives the warm ball more energy to bounce back than the cold ball has.**

What did we learn?

- When is a substance called a gas? **When it has enough energy for the molecules to break apart from each other and move freely.**

- What is the shape of a gas? **It takes on the shape of its container.**

- In which state of matter are the molecules moving the fastest? **In a gas.**

- What is atmospheric pressure? **The pressure applied to a surface by the collision of the air molecules with that surface.**

Taking it further

- How is a gas similar to a liquid? **The molecules of both a gas and a liquid can move around and they both take on the shape of their containers.**

- How is a gas different from a liquid? **Gas molecules have much more energy, they freely move away from each other, and they collide with other molecules and objects billions of times a second. Gas expands to fill its container so it does not have a definite volume.**

- Why is it necessary that a space suit be pressurized in outer space? **God designed our bodies to operate in an environment where there is pressure on our bodies. If this pressure were not there, we would die. Since there is no air in space there is no air pressure, so space suits must provide the pressure necessary for the astronauts.**

15 Gas Laws

Rules to live by

Supply list

Empty 1-gallon milk carton
Balloon
Microwave oven

Cloth tape measure or
    string and a ruler
Access to a freezer

Supplies for Challenge:

Plastic ½-liter or 1-liter bottle
Dish soap   Hot and cold water

What did we learn?

- If temperature remains constant, what happens to the volume of a gas when the pressure is increased? **The volume decreases.**

- If pressure remains constant, what happens to the volume of a gas when the temperature is increased? **The volume increases.**

- What are two different ways to increase the volume of a gas? **Decrease the pressure or increase the temperature.**

Taking it further

- Why might you need to check the air in your bike tires before you go for a ride on a cold day? **The volume of air may be decreased enough by the cold temperatures that you may need to add some air so your tires will not be flat.**

- Why do you think increasing pressure decreases the volume of a gas? **The pressure forces the molecules closer together so they take up less space.**

- Why do you think increasing temperature increases the volume of a gas? **The increase in the temperature adds energy to the molecules causing them to move faster so they spread out more and take up more space.**

- What might happen to the volume of a gas when the pressure is increased and the temperature is increased at the same time? **It depends on how much the pressure and temperature are increased. It is possible that the volume could remain the same. It could also increase or decrease. Because you are changing two things at once, you can't be certain of the effect without knowing how much you are changing each condition.**

QUIZ 3 States of Matter

Lessons 10–15

Use the terms from the list below to fill in the blanks.

1. The three states of matter are _**solid**_, _**liquid**_, and _**gas**_.

2. _**Adding heat**_ causes the molecules in matter to move more quickly.

3. _**Removing heat**_ causes the molecules in matter to move more slowly.

4. _**Removing heat**_ is required to change a gas into a liquid.

5. _**Adding heat**_ is required to change a solid into a liquid.

Write S beside the statement if it describes a property of a solid, L if it describes a liquid, and G if it describes a gas. Some statements describe more than one state of matter.

6. _**S, L**_ Molecules are close together.

7. _**G**_ Molecules are far apart.

8. _**L, G**_ It takes on the shape of its container.

9. _**G**_ Molecules move very quickly.

10. _**L**_ Molecules slide over each other.

11. _**G**_ Easily compressed.

12. _**S**_ Has a defined shape.

13. _**S, L**_ Has a defined volume.

14. _S_ Molecules only vibrate.

15. _S, L_ Not easily compressed.

Mark each statement as either True or False.

16. _T_ Thick liquids have a high viscosity.

17. _F_ As the temperature of a gas increases, its volume decreases.

18. _T_ As the pressure of a gas increases, its volume decreases.

19. _T_ A ball will usually bounce better on a warm day than on a cold one.

20. _F_ Molecules in a viscous liquid are not strongly attracted to each other.

21. _T_ There is a direct relationship between the temperature of a gas and its volume.

22. _T_ Crystals are more likely to form when a solid cools slowly.

Challenge questions

Mark each statement as either True or False.

23. _T_ Solid water is less dense than liquid water.

24. _T_ Glass can be classified as an amorphous solid.

25. _F_ Evaporation requires that a liquid be heated to the boiling point.

26. _F_ Diffusion occurs as molecules move from an area of lower concentration to an area of higher concentration.

27. _T_ Glass does not have a definite boiling point.

28. _F_ All solids are denser than their liquid form.

29. _F_ Evaporation is slower on windy days.

30. _T_ Increasing surface area increases evaporation rate.

Identify each of the following changes as a chemical change or a physical change.

31. _Physical_ Adding water to orange juice.

32. _Physical_ Shredding a piece of paper.

33. _Chemical_ Taking aspirin for a headache.

34. _Chemical_ Burning a candle

35. _Chemical_ Shooting off fireworks

Unit 4
Classifying Matter

16 Elements

The basic building blocks

Supply list

Jigsaw puzzle

Supplies for Challenge:

Copy of "Learning about the Elements" worksheet

What did we learn?

- What is an element? **It is a substance that cannot be broken down by ordinary chemical means—an atom.**
- What is a compound? **It is a substance that is formed when two or more elements combine chemically—a molecule.**
- What is a mixture? **It is a combination of two or more substances that do not make a new substance.**

Taking it further

- If a new element was discovered and it was named newmaterialium, would you expect it to be a metal or a non-metal? **It would probably be a metal because most metal names end in "um" or "ium."**
- Is salt an element, a compound or a mixture? **Salt is a compound made from sodium and chlorine. It can be broken apart into its elements. But when they are put together they form a new substance.**
- Is a soft drink an element, compound or mixture? **It is a mixture of water, sugar, flavorings, and other substances, but it is not a new substance.**

Challenge: Learning about the Elements worksheet

Name	Symbol	Atomic number
Hydrogen	H	1
Oxygen	O	8
Aluminum	Al	13
Silicon	Si	14
Mercury	Hg	80

Metal	Metalloid	Non-metal
Sodium	Germanium	Nitrogen
Gold	Polonium	Phosphorus
Barium	Arsenic	Fluorine
Potassium	Antimony	Neon
Calcium	Boron	Chlorine
Silver		

Magnesium—12

Sulfur—16

Argon—18

Iron—26

Copper—29

Platinum—78

Bismuth—83

Radon—86

17 Compounds

Making new substances

Supply list

2 small jars (small baby food jars or test tubes)

Copper wire (at least 3 feet)

6-volt battery (big square battery)

Baking soda

Electrolysis of Water

1. What do you think is in each jar? **Students may suggest air. The correct answer is hydrogen in one jar and oxygen in the other.**

2. Which jar do you think has the hydrogen in it? **The jar that has more gas has the hydrogen. Remember, there are 2 hydrogen atoms for every oxygen atom in the water.**

3. Why do you think the battery is needed to separate the atoms? **Energy is required to break the bonds of the molecule, and the battery supplies electrical energy.**

What did we learn?

- What is a compound? **A substance that is formed when two or more different kinds of atoms are chemically joined together.**
- What is another name for an element? **An atom.**
- What is another name for compound? **A molecule.**
- Do compounds behave the same way as the atoms that they are made from? **Not usually. Oxygen gas and hydrogen gas act very differently than liquid water or water vapor.**

Taking it further

- The symbol for carbon dioxide is CO_2. What atoms combine to form this molecule? **One carbon atom and two oxygen atoms.**
- The air consists of nitrogen and oxygen molecules. Is air a compound? Why or why not? **The air is not a compound because the nitrogen and oxygen molecules do not bond with each other to form a different substance. Instead, air is a mixture of gases.**

18 Water

God's compound for life

Supply list

Copy of "Water, Water Everywhere" worksheet

Supplies for Challenge:

Three 2-liter plastic bottles   Bean seeds

Cotton string   Ice water

Potting soil

Water, Water Everywhere worksheet

- **Food, water, beverages, washing dishes, cooking, making ice, growing house plants, water for pets, brushing teeth, toilets, bath/shower, washing hands/face, wiping counters, washing windows, laundry, mopping floors, watering grass, breathing, sweating/cooling your body, digestion, blood circulation, blinking, elimination of wastes, making of new cells, etc.**

What did we learn?

- What two kinds of atoms combine to form water? **Hydrogen and oxygen.**
- Why is water called a universal solvent? **Because a large variety of substances can be dissolved in water.**
- What is unique about the water molecule that makes it able to dissolve so many substances? **The hydrogen atoms attach to the oxygen atom at a 105° angle, causing the charge to be unevenly distributed.**

Taking it further

- What would happen to your body if oxygen could not be dissolved in water? **Your blood would not be able to take oxygen to the cells in your body and you would die.**

- Is water truly a universal solvent? **No, there are many substances, particularly oils and fats, that do not dissolve in water.**

- Why is it important for mothers with nursing babies to drink lots of water? **Water is used in the production of milk.**

Mixtures

All mixed up

Supply list

Coffee filter   Funnel

Orange juice   Cup

What did we learn?

- What are two differences between a compound and a mixture? **A compound is formed when two or more elements combine to form a new substance. A mixture is formed when two or more elements or compounds are combined but do not form a new substance. The elements in a compound are always in the same proportion. The elements or compounds in a mixture can be in any proportion.**

- What is a homogeneous mixture? **One in which all of the substances are evenly distributed.**

- What is a heterogeneous mixture? **One in which all of the substances are not evenly distributed.**

- Name three common mixtures. **Air, milk, granite, orange juice, and seawater.**

Taking it further

- If a soft metal is combined with a gas to form a hard solid that doesn't look or act like either of the original substances, is the resulting substance a mixture or a compound? **The result is a compound because the new substance has different characteristics from the original substances. In a mixture, the substances retain their original properties.**

- How might you separate the salt from the sand and water in a sample of seawater? **First, you could filter out the sand. Then you could let the water evaporate into the air and the salt would be left behind, or you could boil away the water like you did in lesson 10. This is similar to the experiment you did in lesson 6 with sugar and water.**

Challenge: Separating Compounds

Cream and milk: **Centrifuge**

Mud and water: **Decantation or filtering**

Food colors: **Chromatography**

Lemon juice and water: **Evaporation**

Oil and water: **Decantation**

Coffee and coffee grounds: **Filtering or decantation**

Air

What we breathe

Supply list

Candle   Baking soda

Jar   Vinegar

Bottle

What did we learn?

- What is likely the most important element on earth? **Oxygen.**

- What is likely the most important compound on earth? **Water.**
- What is likely the most important mixture on earth? **Air.**
- What are the main components of air? **Oxygen and nitrogen.**

Taking it further

- Why is nitrogen necessary in the air? **Nitrogen dilutes the oxygen. Nitrogen also protects the earth from harmful gamma rays.**

- Why is oxygen necessary in air? **Oxygen is necessary for cellular respiration in all plants and animals. Oxygen also protects the earth from harmful x-rays.**
- How does the composition of air show God's provision for life? **Air provides exactly what is necessary for life without harming life on earth. Air protects living things from harmful radiation. Also ozone, which is poisonous, is only found in the upper atmosphere.**

21 Milk & Cream

Udderly delicious

Supply list

2 cups liquid whipping cream

Jar with lid	Bowl
Sugar	Plate
Vanilla extract	Electric mixer

Canned spray whipping cream (made with real cream)

Supplies for Challenge:

Whole milk	Pan
Vinegar	Access to stove

What did we learn?

- Is milk an element, a compound, or a mixture? **Milk is a mixture.**
- What is pasteurization and why is it used on milk? **Pasteurization is the process of heating the milk to kill the bacteria in it.**

- What is homogenization and why is it done to milk? **Homogenization is the process that breaks the fat molecules into tiny bits so they stay suspended in the milk. This prevents the cream from separating from the milk and floating to the top.**
- What is a foam? **It is a liquid that has air molecules suspended in it.**

Taking it further

- Why does whipped cream begin to "weep"? **The fat molecules lose their ability to keep the lighter air molecules trapped and the air eventually escapes.**
- Why must cream be churned in order to make butter? **To form butter, the fat molecules must be forced together. Churning forces the molecules to clump together.**

Classifying Matter

Lessons 16–21

Match the terms below with their correct definition or description.

1. _C_ A combination of two or more pure substances where each keeps its own properties—a new substance is *not* formed.

2. _J_ A liquid with air bubbles trapped in it.

3. _B_ A substance made when two or more elements combine chemically.

4. _G_ The process of heating a mixture to kill the bacteria in it.

5. _A_ A substance that cannot be broken down chemically.

6. _D_ A mixture where the substances are thoroughly mixed up.

7. _E_ A mixture where the substances are not evenly mixed up.

8. _H_ A nearly universal solvent.

9. _I_ The process of breaking up fat into tiny pieces that can remain suspended.

10. _F_ The ability of fat molecules to keep air molecules suspended.

Short answer:

11. Explain why whipped cream eventually melts into a pool of white liquid? **The fat molecules become unable to hold the gas and it escapes.**

12. Give an example showing that a compound does not act like the elements that it is made from. **Accept any reasonable answer such as liquid water does not act like oxygen gas or hydrogen gas.**

13. Explain why water is considered by many to be a nearly universal solvent. **Most substances will dissolve in water because of its unique shape.**

14. What elements are found in the compound CH_4 **Carbon and hydrogen (1 carbon and 4 hydrogen atoms).**

Challenge questions

15. What is a mineral? **Compound found in earth's crust.**

16. Name three groups of minerals. **Silicates, carbonates, halides, sulfides, phosphates, oxides.**

17. What is a native mineral? **Mineral containing only one element.**

18. List three ways to separate substances in a mixture. **Filtering, decantation, distillation, evaporation, chromatography, centrifuge.**

19. Briefly explain how milk is turned into cheese. **Acid is added to coagulate the milk, curds are separated from the whey, an enzyme is added to harden the curds, curds can be pressed and aged.**

20. What instrument is used to separate blood cells from plasma? **Centrifuge.**

Solutions

22 Solutions

Will it dissolve?

Supply list

Roll of Life Savers candy   Plastic zipper bag

Rolling pin   3 cups

Copy of "Solutions Experiment" worksheet

Supplies for Challenge:

Potassium salt (Potassium chloride)

Table salt (sodium chloride)   Vegetable oil

Sugar   Baking soda

Dish soap   4 clear cups

Copy of "Like Dissolves Like" worksheet

Solutions Experiments worksheet

- **Candy will dissolve fastest in hot water. Crushed candy will dissolve faster than whole candy. Candy will dissolve faster if you move your tongue because moving your tongue brings more saliva molecules in contact with the candy so they have more opportunity to dissolve it.**

What did we learn?

- What is a solution? **A mixture in which one substance is dissolved in another.**

- Is a solution a homogeneous or heterogeneous mixture? **A solution is homogeneous.**

- In a solution, what is the name for the substance being dissolved? **The solute.**

- In a solution, what is the substance called in which the solute is dissolved? **The solvent.**

- What is solubility? **The maximum amount of a substance that can be dissolved in a given amount of solvent.**

Taking it further

- Why can more salt be dissolved in hot water than in cold water? **The warmer molecules are moving faster and can hold more salt molecules away from each other so they can dissolve more salt than the slower, colder water molecules.**

- If you want sweet iced tea, would it be better to add the sugar before or after you cool the tea? **If you add the sugar while the tea is hot you will be able to dissolve more sugar and thus the tea will be sweeter. Whether this is better depends on how sweet you like your tea.**

Like Dissolves Like worksheet

- **Soap is the only one of these substances that will dissolve in the oil because it is the only one that has a similar molecular structure to oil.**

23 Suspensions

And we don't mean getting kicked out of school.

Supply list

1 egg   Salt

Vinegar   Vegetable oil

Dry mustard   Small mixing bowl

Lemon juice   Electric mixer

Paprika

Supplies for Challenge:

Cake mix   Oil

Eggs

Ingredients called for in cake mix

What did we learn?

- What is a suspension? **A suspension is a mixture of substances that don't dissolve. It has particles of one substance that can stay suspended in the other for a short period of time, but not indefinitely.**

- What does immiscible mean? **Two liquids that do not mix are immiscible.**

- What is an emulsifier? **A substance that keeps immiscible liquids suspended.**

- What is a colloid? **A liquid with very tiny particles suspended in it.**

Taking it further

- What would happen to the mayonnaise if the egg yolk was left out of the recipe? **The oil would separate out and it would lose its creamy texture.**

- How is a suspension different from a true solution? **The molecules that are dissolved in a solution will stay dissolved indefinitely, whereas the particles that are suspended will eventually settle out of a suspension if an emulsifier is not added.**

24 Solubility

How well does it dissolve?

Supply list

2 canned soft drinks (1 at room temperature and 1 chilled)

2 clear cups

Supplies for Challenge:

Table salt   Sugar

Potassium salt   4 clear cups

Baking soda

Copy of "Solubility of Various Substances" worksheet

Warm or Cold Solutions

1. What are the main ingredients in the solution you are observing? **Carbon dioxide gas dissolved in water. The solution also contains sugar, but we are interested in observing the gas.**

2. Which cup appears to be more bubbly? **Should be the one with warmer liquid.**

3. Does gas escape more easily from a warm solution or a cold solution? **Warm.**

4. Which cup contains the colder liquid? **The one with fewer escaping bubbles.**

What did we learn?

- What is solubility? **The ability of a solvent to dissolve a solute.**

- What are the three factors that most affect solubility? **The type of materials being dissolved, temperature, and pressure.**

- What is the name given to particles that come out of a saturated solution? **A precipitate or precipitation.**

Taking it further

- Why are soft drinks canned or bottled at low temperatures and high pressure? **Soft drinks are a solution of carbon dioxide dissolved in a liquid. To keep the maximum amount of gas dissolved, the solution is canned or bottled at low temperatures under high pressure.**

- Why do soft drinks eventually go flat once opened? **The pressure has been reduced on the solution so the liquid cannot hold as much gas as it once did. The gas escapes into the air and the drink tastes flat.**

- If no additional sugar has been added to a saturated solution of sugar water, what can you conclude about the temperature and/or pressure if you notice sugar beginning to settle on the bottom of the cup? **You can conclude that the temperature of the solution has dropped.**

Solubility of Various Substances worksheet

- **Sugar has the highest solubility; baking soda has the lowest solubility.**

25 Soft Drinks

America's (second) favorite drink

Supply list

Club soda

Orange juice

Sugar or corn syrup

Measuring spoons

Food coloring (yellow, red, blue)

Baking soda

Vanilla extract

Nutmeg

Cinnamon

Lemon juice

Supplies for Challenge:

Cans of regular and diet soft drinks (same brand and flavor)

What did we learn?

- What are the main ingredients of soft drinks? **Water, sweetener, flavoring, color, and carbon dioxide.**

- What is the most popular drink in the United States? The second most popular? **Water, followed in second place by soft drinks.**

- What are the two most popular sweeteners used in soft drinks? **Corn syrup and aspartame.**

Taking it further

- Why are soft drink cans warmed and dried before they are boxed? **The drink is very cold when it is canned or bottled. As it warms up, water condenses on the outside of the can or bottle. If this occurred after packaging, the water would make the boxes or cartons soggy, so it is done beforehand.**

- Why are recipes for soft drinks considered top secret? **People buy a particular brand of soft drink because they like that flavor better than any other. So if someone obtained a secret recipe, the original company could lose money.**

- Why would the finished syrup be tested before adding the carbonation? **To ensure that it tastes correctly before it completes the process; to make sure that nothing went wrong in the previous steps.**

26 Concentration

Is your lemonade weak?

Supply list

Milk

Ice

Sugar

Quart-sized plastic zipper bag

Sandwich-sized plastic zipper bag

Salt

Vanilla extract

Supplies for Challenge:

Thermometer

Stopwatch

Sauce pan

Copy of "Salt's Effect on the Freezing and Boiling Point of Water" worksheet

Baking soda

2 cups

Saltwater

Access to stove

What did we learn?

- What is a dilute solution? **One in which there are relatively few solute molecules in the solution.**

- What is a concentrated solution? **One in which there are a relatively large number of solute molecules in the solution.**

- How does the concentration of a solution affect its boiling point? **In general, the more concentrated it is, the higher the boiling point will be.**

- How does the concentration of a solution affect its freezing point? **In general, the more concentrated it is, the lower the freezing point will be.**

Taking it further

- Why is a quantitative observation for concentration usually more useful than a qualitative observation? **Qualitative observations are based on people's perceptions and not easily repeated. One person may think that the lemonade is too strong while another thinks it is too weak. But quantitative observations are not a matter of opinion and can be repeated.**

- If a little antifreeze helps an engine run better, would it be better to add straight antifreeze to the radiator? **Not necessarily. The combination of different molecules raises the boiling point and lowers the freezing point of both substances in the solution, but straight antifreeze would not necessarily have the same effect.**

Challenge: Salt's Effect on the Freezing and Boiling Point of Water worksheet

- **You should find that salt increases the boiling point and decreases the freezing point of water.**

27 Seawater

The world's most common solution

Supply list

Water   Salt

Soda straw   Egg

What did we learn?

- What is the most common solution on earth? **Seawater.**

- What are the main elements found in the ocean besides water? **Sodium chloride—salt, magnesium, and bromine.**

- How does salt get into the ocean? **Water flowing over land dissolves salt and other minerals and carries them to the ocean. The minerals stay behind when the water evaporates.**

- Name one gas that is dissolved in the ocean water. **Oxygen is the main gas. Nitrogen, carbon dioxide, and other gases are present as well.**

Taking it further

- Why is seawater saltier than water in the rivers and lakes? **Fresh water is continually entering and exiting the rivers and lakes. So the amount of salt remains low. However, in the ocean, the only way that water leaves is through evaporation, which removes the water but leaves the minerals. After thousands of years, the salt has built up in the oceans.**

- Why is there more oxygen near the surface of the ocean than in deeper parts? **Algae and other plants grow near the surface and produce oxygen that dissolves in the water.**

28 Water Treatment

Making it clean

Supply list

Empty 2-liter plastic bottle	2 cups
Dirt	Dish or tray
Sand	Charcoal briquettes
Gravel or small pebbles	Plastic zipper bag
Alum	Cotton balls
Hammer	Goggles

What did we learn?

- Why do we need water treatment plants? **Water from rivers and lakes contains dirt, harmful bacteria, and other substances that are not healthy for people to drink.**

- What are the three main things that are done to water to make it clean enough for human consumption? **Particles are allowed to settle out, chemicals are added to kill bacteria, and the water is filtered.**

- Why is it important not to dump harmful chemicals into rivers and lakes? **The chemicals will dissolve in the water and harm the plants and animals living there.**

Taking it further

- How is the filter you built similar to God's design for cleaning the water? **Much of the water that falls on the earth sinks into the ground where it flows through sand and gravel and becomes cleaner before reaching rivers and underground water tables.**

Solutions

Lessons 22–28

Mark each statement as either True or False.

1. _T_ All solutions are mixtures.
2. _F_ All mixtures are solutions.
3. _F_ A saturated solution can dissolve more solute.
4. _T_ True solutions do not settle out.
5. _F_ Milk is a true solution.
6. _T_ Temperature affects how fast substances dissolve.
7. _T_ Surface area affects how fast substances dissolve.
8. _F_ A dilute solution has a high amount of solute.
9. _T_ The boiling point of a solution is affected by concentration.
10._T_ Cold liquids can suspend more gas than warmer liquids.

Short answer:

11. Describe why decreasing temperature decreases the solubility of a solid in a liquid. **Decreasing the temperature causes the solvent molecules to move more slowly so they cannot keep as many solute molecules separated as they could when they were moving more quickly.**

12. Describe why increased pressure increases the solubility of a gas in a liquid. **Pressure pushes the molecules closer together so the gas molecules cannot escape as easily.**

13. What is a precipitate? **It is a dissolved substance that comes out of the saturated solution.**

14. Why is salt added to ice when freezing ice cream? **Salt lowers the freezing point of the ice, allowing it to absorb more heat from the ice cream mixture and thus making the cream freeze more quickly.**

15. What is likely to happen to a car without antifreeze in the radiator? **The water will boil more easily and could boil over if the temperatures get high. Also, water will freeze more easily and could freeze in the winter time.**

Challenge questions

Short answer:

16. If a substance easily dissolves in water would you expect it to easily dissolve in oil? **It is not likely since like dissolves like and water and oil are very different.**

17. Why does soap easily dissolve in both water and oil? **Soap is a unique molecule that is shaped similarly to water on one end and similarly to oil on the other end.**

18. Name one commercial application for an emulsion. **Foods such as mayonnaise, lotions, paints, espresso, photographic film.**

19. How does the concentration of salt affect the boiling point of water? **As salt concentration goes up so does the boiling point.**

20. Why does salt affect the boiling point this way? **The salt molecules prevent the water molecules from reaching the surface and escaping into the air so more energy is needed to bring the solution to a boil.**

21. How does temperature affect the density of sea water? **The colder the water, the closer together the molecules are so the denser it will be. This is true as long as the water does not freeze.**

22. Why is hard water considered a problem? **Hard water can cause soap scum to form on clothes, dishes, and skin. It can cause scaly deposits to build up in pipes and water heaters.**

Food Chemistry

29 Food Chemistry

You are what you eat

Supply list

Ingredients to make your favorite cookies

Supplies for Challenge:

Research materials on food chemicals

Copy of "Food Chemicals" worksheet

What did we learn?

- What are the three main types of chemicals that naturally occur in food? **Carbohydrates, proteins, and fats.**
- What kinds of chemicals are often added to foods? **Preservatives, flavor enhancers, and color enhancers.**
- Why is the kitchen a great place to look for chemicals? **All of our foods are made of chemicals, and many chemical reactions occur as we are cooking.**

Taking it further

- If you eat a peanut butter and jelly sandwich, which part of the sandwich will be providing the most carbohydrates? The most fat? The most protein? **The bread will provide the most carbohydrates, although it depends on how much jelly you put on. Jelly is mostly** sugar, which is also a carbohydrate. The peanut butter will provide nearly all of the fat and most of the protein.

Challenge: Food Chemicals worksheet

1. What chemical is found in coffee and soft drinks that interferes with some people falling asleep? **Caffeine.**
2. What is the chemical name for table sugar? **Sucrose.**
3. What is the chemical name for baking soda? **Sodium bicarbonate.**
4. What is the chemical name for table salt? **Sodium chloride.**
5. What chemical makes you cry when you slice onions? **Sulfuric acid.**
6. What chemical gives peppers their hot flavor? **Capsaicin.**
7. What chemical gives carrots their orange color? **Carotene.**
8. What chemical gives tomatoes their red color? **Lycopene.**
9. What chemical gives broccoli its green color? **Chlorophyll.**
10. What chemical gives a soft drink its bubbles? **Carbon dioxide.**

30 Chemical Analysis of Food

How do I know what I'm eating?

Supply list

Copy of "Chemical Analysis" worksheet

Iodine

Potato or tortilla chips

Apple slices

Brown paper bag

Bread

Flour

Vegetable oil

Peanut butter

Supplies for Challenge:

Copy of "How Many Calories Did I Eat?" worksheet

Copy of "Calories Chart"

Chemical Analysis worksheet

- **Vegetable oil, peanut butter, and chips should all have turned the paper translucent since these foods are high in fat/oil. Depending on the type of bread you used you may have detected a small amount of oil.**

- **Bread, corn, potatoes, and flour are all high in starch and should have changed color when combined with iodine.**

- **Water does not contain any fats or starches so should not have reacted in either test. Apples contain a high amount of sugar but very little fat and starch so should not have reacted in either test.**

What did we learn?

- What are the main chemicals listed on food labels? **Carbohydrates such as sugar and starch, proteins, fats, vitamins, and minerals.**

- How do food manufacturers know what to put on their labels? **Chemists have tested the foods to see what they are composed of.**

- What is one way to test if a food contains oil? **Place a sample on brown paper for a few minutes and see if it makes the paper become translucent.**

- What is an indicator? **A substance that is used to detect the presence of a particular chemical, usually by changing color.**

Taking it further

- How do you suppose indicators work? **Usually the indicator molecules react with the desired chemical to produce a substance that is a different color from the indicator. For example, iodine turns blue in the presence of starch molecules because of a chemical reaction with the starch that produces a blue substance.**

- Why is it important to know what chemicals are in our food? **This information allows us to compare different foods and decide which ones are best to eat. Also, some people are allergic to particular foods and food labels help them avoid those foods.**

31 Flavors

Chocolate or vanilla?

Supply list

Roll of Life Savers candies

Instant pudding (your favorite flavor)

Milk

What did we learn?

- What two parts of your body are needed in order to fully enjoy the flavor of your food? **The taste buds in your mouth and the smell receptors in your nose.**

- What is the difference between an herb and a spice? **Herbs come from the leaves of a plant; spices come from other parts of the plant.**

- What is the difference between a natural flavor and an artificial flavor? **Natural flavors come directly from a plant. Artificial flavors are created by combining chemicals in a lab or factory.**

Taking it further

- Why might a cook prefer to use fresh herbs rather than dried herbs? **Fresh herbs usually have a milder flavor than dried herbs. However, fresh herbs can spoil more quickly than dried herbs.**

- Why do you think artificial vanilla tastes different than natural vanilla even though they may have the same chemical formula? **Flavor is a complicated thing. Scientists are not quite sure how the flavors are changed, but artificial flavors often produce an unpleasant or bitter aftertaste that natural flavors do not have.**

32 Additives

What's really in your food?

Supply list

Apple   Lemon juice

Supplies for Challenge:

Copy of "Food Additives Checklist" worksheet

What did we learn?

- What is a food additive? **Anything that is added to the food by a manufacturer.**
- Name three different kinds of additives. **Preservatives, antioxidants, emulsifiers, stabilizers, coloring, flavor enhancers, vitamins, and minerals.**
- Why are preservatives sometimes added to foods? **To keep the foods from spoiling.**

- What compound has been used as a preservative for thousands of years? **Salt has been used to preserve many foods, especially meats. Sugar has also been used for a long time.**
- Why are emulsifiers sometimes added to foods? **To keep the oil and water in the foods from separating. Remember when you made mayonnaise?**

Taking it further

- Why are vitamins and minerals added to foods? **Processing, such as heating, often kills bacteria but also destroys many of the nutrients in the foods. Vitamins and minerals are often added back in to restore the nutritional value of the food.**
- Why does homemade bread spoil faster than store bought bread? **Because it does not contain preservatives like the store bought bread does.**

33 Bread

Why is it light and fluffy?

Supply list

Flour	Sugar
Butter or margarine	Baking pan
Yeast	Spray oil
Water	Large bowl
Salt	Small bowl
Milk	

Supplies for Challenge:

Store-bought bread (with preservatives)
Plastic zipper bags
Copy of "Homemade vs. Store-bought" worksheet

What did we learn?

- If you want fluffy bread, what are the two most important ingredients? **Wheat flour that contains gluten, and yeast.**

- Why is gluten important for fluffy bread? **The gluten allows the bread dough to stretch and traps the gas produced by the yeast.**
- Why does bread have to be baked before you eat it? **The baking process breaks down the long starch molecules into smaller molecules that are more easily digested.**
- Why is whole wheat bread more nutritious than white bread? **The white flour does not contain all of the parts of the wheat kernel, so it has fewer nutrients.**

Taking it further

- What would happen if you did not put any sugar in your bread dough? **The yeast would not be able to produce as much carbon dioxide gas, so your bread would not be as fluffy.**
- Can bread be made without yeast? **Yes, other forms of leavening can be used such as baking soda or baking powder. However, the bread will be more like tortillas or pita bread than the fluffy bread you may be used to.**

Challenge: Homemade vs. Store-bought worksheet

- Homemade bread in general will dry out faster and will grow more mold than store-bought bread. However, you may prefer the flavor of homemade bread. Also, homemade bread my be more nutritious.

QUIZ 6 — Food Chemistry

Lessons 29–33

Choose the best answer for each question.

1. _B_ Which is the most popular drink in the world?
2. _A_ What are 70% of all soft drinks sweetened with?
3. _D_ To guarantee that each soft drink tastes the same, what must a company do?
4. _D_ Which of the following is not used to make soft drinks?
5. _D_ What accounts for the perceived flavor of a food?
6. _B_ Which civilization is believed to be the first to enjoy chocolate?
7. _C_ What is the purpose of fermenting vanilla beans?
8. _B_ Which of the following is a natural flavor?
9. _A_ How do additives help preserve food?
10. _C_ Which of the following helps bread to be fluffy?
11. _B_ Which agency oversees the use of food additives?
12. _C_ Which of the following makes bread easier to digest?

Challenge questions

13. _D_ Which chemical is the name for table sugar?
14. _C_ Which chemical gives tomatoes their red color?
15. _A_ A calorimeter measures energy in food by _burning_ it.
16. _B_ Flavor is combination of _taste and smell_.
17. _B_ Food additives usually are not used for _calories_.
18. _B_ Approximately how many Calories does a teenager need each day?

34 — Identification of Unknown Substances

What is this, anyway?

Final Project supply list

Copy of "Identification of Solids" worksheet
Copy of "Identification of Liquids" worksheet

Iodine	Cornstarch
Vinegar	Rubbing alcohol
Baking soda	Powdered sugar
Water	Vegetable oil

Final Project instructions

Set up each of the following experiments. Have your students write their observations on copies of the "Identification of Solids" and "Identification of Liquids" worksheets.

- **Experiment 1:** Number three plates or other containers with the numbers 1–3. On plate 1 place two tablespoons of cornstarch. On plate 2 place two tablespoons of powdered sugar. On plate 3 place two tablespoons of baking soda. Do not tell your student which substance is which until after he/she has done the experiments on the worksheet. You may give younger children a list of substances from which to choose.

- **Experiment 2:** Number three cups 1–3. Place ½ cup of water in cup 1. Place ½ cup of vinegar in cup 2. Place ½ cup of rubbing alcohol in cup 3. Again, do not tell your student which substance is which until he/she has done the experiments on the worksheet.

Again, you may want to give younger children a list of possible choices.

What did we learn?

- What method should be used in identifying unknown substances? **The scientific method.**
- Why should you avoid tasting unknown substances? **The substance can be dangerous or harmful, so you don't want to taste it if you don't know what it is.**
- How can you test the scent of an unknown substance safely? **Hold it a few inches away from your nose and push some air toward your nose. This allows you to smell a few molecules without damaging your nose if the scent is very strong or caustic, like ammonia.**

- What are some physical characteristics of an unknown substance you can test at home? **Mass, density, melting point, freezing point, boiling point, and state—such as solid, liquid, or gas.**
- What are some chemical characteristics you can test at home? **Presence of starch, oil, baking powder, acid or base.**

Taking it further

- Why is it important for food manufacturers to test the ingredients they use and final products they produce? **To ensure the safety and flavor of their foods.**
- Why is it important for water treatment facilities to test the quality of the water? **We don't want harmful bacteria or other dangerous substances in our water supply.**

Properties of Matter

Lessons 1–34

Use the terms below to fill in the blanks.

1. How much of a substance you have is its _**mass**_.
2. How much space something occupies is its _**volume**_.
3. How much gravity pulls on a mass is its _**weight**_.
4. The three states of matter are _**solid**_, _**liquid**_, and _**gas**_.
5. When a liquid changes to a gas it is called _**evaporation**_.
6. When a solid changes to a liquid it is called _**melting**_.
7. When a liquid changes to a solid it is called _**freezing**_.
8. When a gas changes to a liquid it is called _**condensation**_.
9. When a solid changes directly to a gas it is called _**sublimation**_.
10. The thickness of a liquid is called its _**viscosity**_.

Match the type of quantitate measurement with the proper tool.

11. _**B**_ Volume of a liquid
12. _**D**_ Mass
13. _**C**_ Weight
14. _**E**_ Temperature
15. _**A**_ Volume of a cube

For each characteristic or statement, put E if it describes an element, C if it describes a compound, or M if it describes a mixture. Some statements have more than one answer.

16. Cannot be broken by ordinary chemical processes. _**E**_
17. Contains two or more kinds of atoms. _**C, M**_
18. Always has the same ratio of elements. _**E, C**_
19. Iron _**E**_
20. Water _**C**_
21. Helium _**E**_
22. Air _**M**_
23. Seawater _**M**_
24. Only 92 of these occur in nature. _**E**_
25. Almost all substances on earth are these. _**M**_

Identify each of the following changes as either a physical change (P) or a chemical change (C).

26. Burning of a candle _**C**_
27. Rusting metal _**C**_
28. Freezing of water _**P**_
29. Crushing a graham cracker _**P**_
30. Combining oxygen and hydrogen to make water _**C**_
31. Rain falling from the clouds _**P**_

Identify each characteristic as describing either a gas, a liquid, or a solid. Some statements have more than one answer.

32. Molecules are far apart. _Gas_.

33. Has a definite shape. _Solid_.

34. Easily compressed. _Gas_.

35. Takes on the shape of its container. _Liquid, gas_.

36. Molecules are very close together. _Solid, liquid_.

37. Molecules slide over one another. _Liquid_.

Short answer:

38. If a liquid is cooled will it be able to dissolve more or fewer solids? **Fewer.**

39. If a soft drink is very bubbly looking is it more likely to be warm or cold? **Warm.**

40. What similar processes are required to produce the flavors of vanilla and chocolate? **Both require fermenting, aging, and drying.**

41. How can you tell if a solution is saturated? **No more solute will dissolve.**

42. How can you tell if a liquid mixture is a solution or a suspension? **If it is a suspension, particles will settle on the bottom; if it is a solution, there will be no settling.**

Challenge questions

Identify each statement as origins or operational science.

43. _Operational_ The melting point of copper is 1084.62°C (1984.32°F).

44. _Origins_ All birds had a common reptile ancestor.

45. _Operational_ Horses give birth to horses.

46. List three different scales used to measure different kinds of storms. **Beaufort—wind; Fujita—tornado; Saffir-Simpson—hurricane**

Mark each statement as either True or False.

47. _F_ An object is denser than another object if it has a greater volume.

48. _F_ Rubbing alcohol is buoyant in water.

49. _T_ Solid water is less dense than liquid water.

50. _T_ Dissolving salt in water is a physical change.

51. _T_ During diffusion, molecules move from an area of higher concentration to an area of lower concentration.

52. _F_ A native mineral has two kinds of elements in it.

53. _T_ Chromatography uses paper to separate substances in a mixture.

54. _T_ Enzymes are used to harden cheese curds.

55. _F_ A centrifuge uses evaporation to separate substances in a mixture.

Match each word with its definition.

56. _C_ Amount of salt in a solution

57. _D_ Water containing calcium and magnesium

58. _F_ Energy to raise 1g of water 1 degree C.

59. _E_ 1000 calories (kilocalorie)

60. _B_ Flavor enhancer

61. _A_ Prevents reacting with oxygen

35 Conclusion

A reliable world

Supply list

2 balloons   Candle

Water   Matches or lighter

What did we learn?

• What is the best thing you learned about matter? **Answers will vary.**

Taking it further

• What else would you like to know about matter? **Go to the library and learn about it.**

Resource Guide

Many of the following titles are available from Answers in Genesis (www.AnswersBookstore.com).

Suggested Books

Structure of Matter by Mark Galan in the *Understanding Science and Nature* series from Time-Life Books—Lots of real-life applications of chemistry

Inventions and Inventors series from Grolier Educational—Many interesting articles

Molecules by Janice VanCleave—Fun activities

Chemistry for Every Kid by Janice VanCleave—More fun activities

Science Lab in a Supermarket by Bob Friedhoffer—Fun kitchen chemistry

Science and the Bible by Donald B. DeYoung—Great biblical applications of scientific ideas

200 Gooey, Slippery, Slimy, Weird & Fun Experiments by Janice VanCleave—More fun activities

Elements of Faith by Richard Duncan— meaningful insights and spiritual applications from the periodic table of the elements

Suggested Videos

Newton's Workshop by Moody Institute—Excellent Christian science series; several titles to choose from

Field Trip Ideas

- Visit the Creation Museum in Petersburg, Kentucky
- Visit a greenhouse or hydroponics operation to see the use of chemicals with plants
- Tour a battery store to learn about different types of batteries
- Visit a film processing plant to learn about chemicals in film processing or photo printing
- Visit a pharmacy
- Tour an injection molding plant to learn more about plastics
- Visit a farm to learn about the use of chemicals in farming

Creation Science Resources

Exploring the World Around You by Gary Parker—More detailed look at different aspects of ecology

Answers Book for Kids Four volumes by Ken Ham with Cindy Malott—Answers children's frequently asked questions

Creation: Facts of Life by Gary Parker—Good explanation of the evidence for creation

The Young Earth by John D. Morris PhD—Evidence for a young earth

The New Answers Books 1–4 by Ken Ham and others—Answers frequently asked questions

Zoo Guide and *Aquarium Guide* by Answers in Genesis—A biblical look at animals, including extinction, defense/attack structures, biomes, and stewardship

Master Supply List

The following table lists all the supplies used for *God's Design for Chemistry & Ecology: Properties of Atoms & Molecules* activities. You will need to look up the individual lessons in the student book to obtain the specific details for the individual activities (such as quantity, color, etc.). The letter *c* denotes that the lesson number refers to the challenge activity. Common supplies such as colored pencils, construction paper, markers, scissors, tape, etc., are not listed.

Supplies needed (see lessons for details)	Lesson
Alum (in spice section)	28
Baking soda	6c, 10, 17, 20, 22c, 24c, 25, 29, 34
Balloon (helium-filled, optional)	9c
Balloons (latex)	2, 6c, 15, 35
Battery (6-volt)	17
Bean seeds	18c
Block (wooden)	12
Bottle (plastic ½-gallon or 1-liter)	15c, 20
Box (small)	3, 7
Bread	30, 33c
Cake mix	23c
Candle	20, 35
Charcoal briquettes	28
Cinnamon	25
Club soda	25
Coffee filter	19
Corn syrup	25
Cornstarch	34
Cotton balls	28
Cups (clear)	3, 9, 22, 22c, 24, 26c, 28
Cups (paper)	5, 6
Dish soap	13, 15c, 22c
Eggs	23, 23c, 27
Eraser	8c
Flour	30, 33
Food coloring	25

Supplies needed (see lessons for details)	Lesson
Funnel	19
Goggles	28
Golf ball	8
Hammer	28
Hand lotion	13
Hand mirror	11
Hole punch	5
Honey	12, 13
Ice tray	11
Iodine	30, 34
Jar (with lid)	11c, 17, 20, 21
Jigsaw puzzle	16
Lemon juice	10, 23, 25, 32
Life Savers candies (roll)	22, 31
Marbles	8c, 9c
Margarine	1, 33
Meter stick/metric ruler	1, 3, 4, 5, 7
Microscope and slides (optional)	3c
Milk (not skim)	21c, 26, 31, 33
Milk jug (1-gallon)	15
Modeling clay	9, 9c
Molasses	2
Mustard (dry)	23
Oil (spray)	33
Oil (vegetable)	9, 13, 23, 22c, 30, 34
Orange juice	19, 25
Paper bag (brown)	30
Paper clips	4, 5, 8
Paprika	23
Peanut butter	30
Pennies	5, 8
Perfume	14c
Ping-pong ball	8
Plastic bottles (empty 2-liter)	2, 6c, 18c, 28
Plastic tub	9
Plastic zipper bags	22, 26, 28, 33c

Supplies needed (see lessons for details)	Lesson
Popcorn	9
Potassium salt (in spice section)	22c, 24c
Potato or tortilla chips	30
Potting soil	18c
Powdered sugar	34
Pudding mix (instant)	31
Rocks	12, 28
Rolling pin	22
Rubber band	5
Rubbing alcohol	9, 34
Salt	10, 22c, 23, 24c, 26, 26c, 27, 33
Sand	28
Scale (gram)	6c
Silly Putty	12
Soft drink (canned, diet & regular)	24, 25c
Soil	28
Spices (ginger root, mint leaves, cinnamon sticks, allsp ice, cloves, peppermint oil, almond extract, etc.)	25
Spoon (metal)	1, 6, 8c, 12

Supplies needed (see lessons for details)	Lesson
Spoon (wooden)	1
Stopwatch	1, 3, 26c
Straw	27
String	5, 18c
Sugar	2, 21, 22c, 24c, 25, 26, 33
Sugar cubes	6
Tape (masking)	2, 3, 5
Tape measure (cloth)	2, 15c
Telescope (optional)	3c
Tennis ball	3, 7c, 14
Thermometer	2, 3, 26c
Vanilla extract	21, 25, 26
Vinegar	6c, 20, 21c, 23, 34
Whipped cream (spray can)	21
Whipping cream (liquid)	21
Wire (copper)	17
Wrenches (or other metal objects)	9
Yeast	2, 33

Works Cited

Ardley, Meil. *Making Metric Measurements*. New York: Franklin Watts, 1983.

"BHA and BHT." http://chemistry.about.com/library/weekly/aa082101a.htm.

Biddle, Verne. *Chemistry Precision and Design*. Pensacola: A Beka Book Ministry, 1986.

Brice, Raphaelle. *From Oil to Plastic*. New York: Young Discovery Library, 1985.

Busenberg, Bonnie. *Vanilla, Chocolate, and Strawberry, The Story of Your Favorite Flavors*. Minneapolis: Lerner Publications Co., 1994.

"The Chemistry of Cakes." http://www.margarine.org.uk/pg_app2.htm.

Chisholm, Jane, and Mary Johnson. *Introduction to Chemistry*. London: Usborne Publishing, 1983.

Cobb, Vicki. *Chemically Active Experiments You Can Do at Home*. New York: J.B. Lippincott, 1985.

Cooper, Christopher. *Matter*. New York: Dorling Kindersley, 1992.

"Desalination of Water." *Columbia Encyclopedia*. 2000.

DeYoung, Donald B. *Science and the Bible*. Grand Rapids: Baker Books, 1994.

Dineen, Jacqueline. *Plastics*. Hillside: Enslow Publishers Inc., 1988.

Dunsheath, Percy. *Giants of Electricity*. New York: Thomas Y. Crowell Co., 1967.

"Energy Value of Food." http://www.cristina.prof.ufsc.br/digestorio/mcardle_energy_value_food_ch4_connection.pdf.

Erlbach, Arlene. *Soda Pop*. Minneapolis: Lerner Publications Co., 1994.

"Farming, Food and Biotechnology." *Inventions and Inventors*. 2000.

"Fleischmann's Yeast: Best-Ever Breads." Birmingham: Time Inc. Ventures Custom Publishing, 1993.

"The Flour Page." http://www.cookeryonline.com/Bread/flour.html.

Friedhoffer, Bob. *Science Lab in a Supermarket*. New York: Franklin Watts, 1998.

Galan, Mark. *Structure of Matter: Understanding Science and Nature*. Alexandria: Time-Life Books, 1992.

Groleau, Rick. "Buoyancy Brainteasers." http://www.pbs.org/wgbh/nova/lasalle/buoyancy.html.

"History." http://www.breadinfo.com/history.shtml.

"How and Why: Science in the Water." *World Book*. 1998.

"How Does a Water Softener Work?" http://home.howstuffworks.com/question99.htm.

"How Sweet It Is!" http://portal.acs.org/portal/fileFetch/C/CSTA_015104/pdf/CSTA_015104.pdf.

Hughey, Pat. *Scavengers and Decomposers: The Cleanup Crew*. New York: Atheneum, 1984.

Julicher, Kathleen. *Experiences in Chemistry*. Baytown: Castle Heights Press, 1997.

Kuklin, Susan. *Fireworks: the Science, the Art, and the Magic*. New York: Hyperion Books for Children, 1996.

Mebane, Robert C., and Thomas R. Rybolt. *Air and Other Gases*. New York: Twenty-first Century Books, 1995.

"Medicine and Health." *Inventions and Inventors*. 2000.

Morris, John D., Ph.D. *The Young Earth*. Colorado Springs: Master Books, 1992.

Newmark, Ann. *Chemistry*. New York: Dorling Kindersley, 1993.

Nottridge, Rhoda. *Additives*. Minneapolis: Carolrhoda Books Inc., 1993.

Parker, Gary. *Creation: Facts of Life*. Colorado Springs: Master Books, 1994.

Parker, Steve. *Look at Your Body—Digestion*. Brookfield: Copper Beech books, 1996.

"Recipes Around the World." http://www.ivu.org/recipes.

Richards, Jon. *Chemicals and Reactions*. Brookfield: Copper Beech books, 2000.

Saari, Peggy and Stephen Allison, Eds. *Scientists: The Lives and Works of 150 Scientists*. U.X.L An Imprint of Gale, 1996.

Solids, Liquids, and Gases. Ontario Science Center. Toronto: Kids Can Press, 1998.

Stancel, Colette, and Keith Graham. *Biology God's Living Creation Field and Laboratory Manual*. Pensacola: A Beka Books, 1998.

Thomas, Peggy. *Medicines from Nature*. New York: Twenty-First Century Books, 1997.

VanCleave, Janice. *Chemistry for Every Kid*. New York: John Wiley and Sons, Inc., 1989.

VanCleave, Janice. *Molecules*. New York: John Wiley and Sons, Inc., 1993.

Walpole, Brenda. *Water*. Ada, OK: Garrett Educational Corp., 1990.

"William Prout." *Classic Encyclopedia*. http://www.1911encyclopedia.org/William_Prout.

Ziegler, Sandra. *A Visit to the Bakery*. Chicago: Children's Press, 1987.